SOAR
with heart-fullness

keys to a meaningful life

Suzanne Letourneau

Published by Skye Insights Company

Copyrights © 2017 by Suzanne Letourneau
1009-100 County Court Blvd
Brampton, ON L6W 3X1 Canada

Editorial supervision: EditPro, Nancy Hutchins

No part of this publication may be reproduced or transmitted in any form or by any means, mechanical or electronic, including photocopying and recording, or by any information storage and retrieval system, without permission in writing from author or publisher (except by a reviewer, who may quote brief passages and/or show brief video clips in a review).

SOAR WITH HEART-FULLNESS
KEYS TO A MEANINGFUL LIFE

ISBN   978-0-9859538-0-5

Table of Contents

Preface 1

Introduction 5

Chapter 1 - My Plan 13

Chapter 2 - First Quarter 79

Chapter 3 - Second Quarter 83

Chapter 4 - Third Quarter 89

Chapter 5 - Fourth Quarter 95

Chapter 6 - Year End 101

Preface

Why is it that resolutions don't work?
Why is it that resolutions don't work while business plans do?

Let's start with resolutions.

1. We make a list of things we **intend** to do, then we put it aside and don't look at it until the end of the year, if at all. Things like: spend more time with family and/or close friends, be a better listener, become healthier and more fit, be more caring, make work more enjoyable, stick to our resolutions, etc.

2. We make a list of things we **intend** to stop doing or change, we put it aside – we might even hide it somewhere, so nobody can point the finger if we don't succeed – and we hope we can make it happen somehow. Things like: stop smoking, stop drinking, stop lying or cheating, stop spending so much money, stop procrastinating, stop pretending, etc.

Suzanne Letourneau

The common ground here is **intent.** We have the intention of doing or not doing something. But unless we give a big huge **attention to our intention,** it is not going to happen. It's like this beautiful tropical plant that needs water every single day. When we stop watering it for a whole month, it unsurprisingly, dies on us. Intending is like **trying**.

> *"Do or do not. There is no try."*
> ~ *Yoda, Star Wars - Episode V*

Okay. We understand resolutions. But what's this about business plans?

A business plan is a formal **statement** of our business goals. It is the map, the blueprint for how we will get there. This **statement** also includes the reasons, the steps, the strategy to reach these goals. A statement is an **expression** of an idea, followed by **actions**.

Much more powerful, isn't it?

All successful entrepreneurs have created a well thought-out and well defined map to guarantee their success. After all, no one goes into business to fail, right?

Then **why** do we allow failure to happen with our resolutions? **W.H.Y is exactly why**! Because, either way, intention or statement, resolutions or business plans, it all needs a **W.H.Y**.

Wonder - Harmony - Yes

The **W.H.Y** is the reason you get up in the morning. It is this eternal child **wonder** that you carry in your heart and sparkles in your eyes. It is unquestionably what keeps you going when the going gets tough. Remember the words from Billy Ocean's song "When the Going Gets Tough, the Tough Gets Going"? It is what makes you give the best and be the best of who you are. Your **W.H.Y** is the fuel, the energy, the spirit behind everything that you do.

And because you are in **harmony** with that thing you are doing, everything flows.

And, of course – **Yes**, life is good!

Suzanne Letourneau

To SOAR with heart-fullness is about feeling, seeing, hearing and doing the things that are really meaningful. Yet, what does "meaningful" really mean? The interpretation of something meaningful might vary from one person to another.

In my book, *SOAR with Vulnerability,* I say exactly the contrary. "*Meaningful is exactly the same for everybody. **Meaning**-full is about doing a simple action that leaves you feeling full-**filled**. It is when you share something that gives you that inner sense of higher purpose and **all**-ways lifts your heart and uplifts the life of others.*"

Doing something really meaningful doesn't mean that it needs to be something really big and flamboyant. It simply needs to make a positive difference in someone's life: a friend's, a family member's, a colleague's, a stranger's, or someone else that you may not even be aware of. When this happens, you will realize that when you're making a difference in someone's life, it automatically makes a difference in your own life. I wonder why!!!!

We human beings need to be reminded of what's meaningful on a daily basis. Otherwise, we have this big tendency to forget — and let ourselves get caught in busy-ness.

This journal, a heart-fullness *"business plan,"* is here to help you stay focused on your **W.H.Y.**

Introduction

This journal is about connecting with your heart, your vulnerable authenticity, your core.

It is about sharing your truth through daily acts of *Meaningfulness and Gratitude.* This journal works perfectly in harmony with my book *SOAR with Vulnerability - Eleven Insights to the Full Enjoyment of Your Life*. As you share your truth, you will realize that everything you say or do, think or fear, is totally connected to your belief system.

Your belief system is a collection of beliefs that were dumped in your lap by your parents, your teachers, your community, your environment, and your culture – beliefs that you have come to accept as your own. Then, you have your own *private collection* of beliefs: the ones you have fabricated of your own free will. LOL! These beliefs are only the interpretation of multiple stories which you have also created.

SOAR with Heart-fullness

In my book SOAR with Vulnerability, I wrote: *"Beliefs are thoughts that we don't question anymore."* What if, for every thought that you have, or had, you could create a whole new story, and therefore, change your whole belief system? What if you were to start questioning every thought you have, right now? You can begin with questioning your thought about the possibility of questioning every thought you have.

To get you going, for each day of this journal, I will share some of the quotes from my book *SOAR with Vulnerability*, along with questions. For each quote, write your takeaway on it, and create your own quote on the topic.

The questions are meant to *be lived*, versus answered. What does that mean? The heart and the mind speak different languages, and both have value in their individual kingdoms. For the purpose of this journal, I will ask you to live – feel, sense, experience, watch – and answer these questions from your heart, versus your mind, because the language of love is much closer to your true nature.

How to use this journal?

Suzanne Letourneau

Let's start by using the word COMMITMENT versus intention, resolution or statement. A <u>commitment is a choice</u>. Therefore, when you commit, it indicates that you are already ENGAGED. So once again, a lot more powerful, right?

This journal is here to help you take the time you need to feel and weigh each one of your commitments. Therefore, instead of writing a long list of resolutions that you intend to accomplish this year, just take one day at a time for the next 31 days and write what you are committing yourself to, on that particular day.

Doing this exercise in the morning is the best. It puts you in the mood for the rest of the day. And don't forget, these commitments are yours, no one else's. You only need to be accountable to *your-self.*

To succeed with your commitments, you need to give them consistent attention. At the end of your first 31 days, return to Day 1 and repeat the cycle, day by day. That means, that every first of the month you return to Day 1 in your journal. You do not need to rewrite anything, but you do need to carefully read your commitment, be with it, feel it, live it and then

SOAR with Heart-fullness

go on with your day, filled with that awesome feeling that you are doing something really meaningful for yourself. Most importantly, though, don't let anything or anyone distract you from your mission for those next 24 hours.

For the months when there are only 30 or 29 days, take out one or two of the commitments that you have already mastered for the previous month.

But before getting started, let's once again look at what I mean by meaningful.

> *"Meaning-full is doing a simple action*
> *that leaves you feeling full-filled.*
> *It is when giving and receiving become one*
> *and the same."*
> *~From SOAR with Vulnerability*

So, to begin...

1. I invite you to question each quote and write your own take on it. Once that is done, decide on a *meaning*-full action that you will do on that particular day, something that is in line with the quote.

2. I invite you to read each question and live the question by moving it into your heart. Then, answer the question. Some questions will appear lighter than others. Don't let it fool you. This is when you need to dig deeper into your vulnerable authenticity, your sensitivity, your openness.

This journal is meant to be used as a heart-*fullness business plan* for the next twelve months from the time you open it. It doesn't have to be from January 1 to December 31. It can be from May 1 to April 30 of the following year. So, whenever you choose to start, yes?

In business we do quarterly reviews to make sure the business is on track with planning, financial forecasts, and anticipated results. When it's not, we need to make adjustments with what works and what doesn't and review the action plan and see what steps are not working and why it is not performing. If it is on track, we still need to look at the performance of all the components and evaluate the ones we are keeping, altering, changing or not touching.

The lined spaced for each commitment should be enough space to write your own quote, or your

SOAR with Heart-fullness

answer to the question, the meaningful action you will take, and of course your WHY. If you do not have enough space, by all means, add extra paper and let the juices flow! This will create the necessary introspection moment for you to see if you have kept your promise to yourself.

If you get stuck, please don't hesitate to get in touch with me at suzanne@suzanneletourneau.com. In the subject line of the email just write "SOAR with heart-fullness" and I will get back to you with dates and time when I can offer you a complimentary strategy session.

Finding the keys to your meaningful life is the key!

Chapter 1

My Plan

Day 1. Vulnerability is about choosing to be free, by being authentic and transparent to yourself and others. What will I do today to embrace my vulnerability, to authentically invite *love* into my life?

My answer/quote:

_____
_____
_____
_____
_____
_____
_____
_____

My meaningful action:

_____
_____
_____
_____
_____
_____
_____
_____

Suzanne Letourneau

My WHY:

_____
_____
_____
_____
_____
_____
_____
_____

SOAR with Heart-fullness

Day 2. Passion is about making a legendary difference in people's lives by sharing your unique gifts. Which one of my unique gifts am I willing to share right now?

My answer/quote:

_____
_____
_____
_____
_____
_____
_____
_____

My meaningful action:

_____
_____
_____
_____
_____
_____
_____

Suzanne Letourneau

My WHY:

_____

_____

_____

_____

_____

_____

_____

_____

SOAR with Heart-fullness

Day 3. You can change just one thing about the world today. What will it be?

My answer/quote:

_____
_____
_____
_____
_____
_____
_____
_____

My meaningful action:

_____
_____
_____
_____
_____
_____
_____
_____

Suzanne Letourneau

My WHY:

_____
_____
_____
_____
_____
_____
_____
_____

SOAR with Heart-fullness

Day 4. You are only invulnerable when you are in fear. What am I afraid of? What will I do today to change that?

My answer/quote:

_____
_____
_____
_____
_____
_____
_____
_____

My meaningful action:

_____
_____
_____
_____
_____
_____
_____
_____

Suzanne Letourneau

My WHY:

_____
_____
_____
_____
_____
_____
_____
_____

SOAR with Heart-fullness

Day 5. Humi*liation* is a feeling. Humi*lity* is being. Can you feel how humility reunites and how humiliation divides? What will I do today in complete humility?

My answer/quote:

_____
_____
_____
_____
_____
_____
_____
_____

My meaningful action:

_____
_____
_____
_____
_____
_____
_____

Suzanne Letourneau

My WHY:

_____
_____
_____
_____
_____
_____
_____
_____

SOAR with Heart-fullness

Day 6. How do I define living, versus being alive?
(Take your time on this one.)

My answer/quote:

_____
_____
_____
_____
_____
_____
_____
_____

My meaningful action:

_____
_____
_____
_____
_____
_____
_____
_____

Suzanne Letourneau

My WHY:

_____
_____
_____
_____
_____
_____
_____
_____

SOAR with Heart-fullness

Day 7. Invulnerability attracts invulnerability. Fear attracts fear. Love attracts love. Vulnerability creates open hearts. Whom do I know in my immediate surroundings who could do with a little bit more love today? What will I do differently today so this person feels the love surrounding her/him?

My answer/quote:

_____
_____
_____
_____
_____
_____
_____

My meaningful action:

_____
_____
_____
_____
_____
_____

Suzanne Letourneau

My WHY:

_____
_____
_____
_____
_____
_____
_____
_____

SOAR with Heart-fullness

Day 8. We have the ability to hear each one of our thoughts. What am I going to do with the ones that are limiting me? (Be specific.)

My answer/quote:

_____
_____
_____
_____
_____
_____
_____
_____

My meaningful action:

_____
_____
_____
_____
_____
_____
_____
_____

Suzanne Letourneau

My WHY:

_____
_____
_____
_____
_____
_____
_____
_____

SOAR with Heart-fullness

Day 9. Mindfulness. It is not about being in our mind. It is about being in full awareness in the moment. What can I do today to remind myself *to be and stay* in the moment, no matter what happens?

My answer/quote:

_____
_____
_____
_____
_____
_____
_____
_____

My meaningful action:

_____
_____
_____
_____
_____
_____
_____

Suzanne Letourneau

My WHY:

_____
_____
_____
_____
_____
_____
_____
_____

SOAR with Heart-fullness

Day 10. Do I prefer to be liked or respected? *(This is one of those questions that seem so easy to answer. Take your time and dig deep.)* How do I feel when people like me and don't necessarily respect me, versus how I feel when people respect me and don't necessarily like me?

My answer/quote:

_____
_____
_____
_____
_____
_____
_____

My meaningful action:

_____
_____
_____
_____
_____
_____

Suzanne Letourneau

My WHY:

_____

_____

_____

_____

_____

_____

_____

_____

SOAR with Heart-fullness

Day 11. Many of us tend to take for granted the greatness that is already present in our lives. When was the last time I noticed and appreciated my daily gifts? How will I express my gratitude today?

My answer/quote:

_____
_____
_____
_____
_____
_____
_____
_____

My meaningful action:

_____
_____
_____
_____
_____
_____
_____

Suzanne Letourneau

My WHY:

_____
_____
_____
_____
_____
_____
_____
_____
_____

SOAR with Heart-fullness

Day 12. If each one of my friends represent a world in me, how will I prepare myself to travel around the world? (*another deep one*)

My answer/quote:

_____
_____
_____
_____
_____
_____
_____
_____

My meaningful action:

_____
_____
_____
_____
_____
_____
_____
_____

Suzanne Letourneau

My WHY:

_____
_____
_____
_____
_____
_____
_____
_____

SOAR with Heart-fullness

Day 13. Whining. Look at the actual reality versus your belief about the reality. What is the reality of my situation?

My answer/quote:

_____
_____
_____
_____
_____
_____
_____
_____

My meaningful action:

_____
_____
_____
_____
_____
_____
_____
_____

Suzanne Letourneau

My WHY:

_____
_____
_____
_____
_____
_____
_____
_____

SOAR with Heart-fullness

Day 14. True listening. Deep and meaningful sharing requires total listening. How will I shift my attention to *attentive*?

My answer/quote:

_____
_____
_____
_____
_____
_____
_____

My meaningful action:

_____
_____
_____
_____
_____
_____
_____
_____

My WHY:

_____
_____
_____
_____
_____
_____
_____
_____

SOAR with Heart-fullness

Day 15. What is holding me back from doing the things I really want to do? *(Dig deep. Don't stop at excuses. Dare to face the truth and, question that truth.)*

My answer/quote:

_____
_____
_____
_____
_____
_____
_____
_____

My meaningful action:

_____
_____
_____
_____
_____
_____
_____

Suzanne Letourneau

My WHY:

_____
_____
_____
_____
_____
_____
_____

SOAR with Heart-fullness

Day 16. Do I find it easier to love or to be loved? And why?

My answer/quote:

_____
_____
_____
_____
_____
_____
_____
_____

My meaningful action:

_____
_____
_____
_____
_____
_____
_____
_____

Suzanne Letourneau

My WHY:

_____
_____
_____
_____
_____
_____
_____
_____

SOAR with Heart-fullness

Day 17. From the moment you start describing the sunset, and saying how beautiful it is, you have left reality and moved into your stories. *(Become a witness of yourself watching the sunset.)*

My answer/quote:

_____
_____
_____
_____
_____
_____
_____
_____

My meaningful action:

_____
_____
_____
_____
_____
_____
_____

Suzanne Letourneau

My WHY:

_____

_____

_____

_____

_____

_____

_____

_____

SOAR with Heart-fullness

Day 18. We all try to cover our fears. But they are always there beneath the surface, with the ego. *(Fear and ego are one and the same.)* The only way you can be without fear, is to accept your fear when it is present. Then ask yourself, who would I be without that fear?

My answer/quote:

_____
_____
_____
_____
_____
_____
_____
_____

My meaningful action:

_____
_____
_____
_____
_____
_____

Suzanne Letourneau

My WHY:

_____
_____
_____
_____
_____
_____
_____
_____

SOAR with Heart-fullness

Day 19. In emptiness lies your fullness. In order to feel this fullness, one needs to surrender. What will I surrender to, today?

My answer/quote:

_____
_____
_____
_____
_____
_____
_____
_____

My meaningful action:

_____
_____
_____
_____
_____
_____
_____
_____

Suzanne Letourneau

My WHY:

_____
_____
_____
_____
_____
_____
_____
_____

SOAR with Heart-fullness

Day 20. Once you let go of the thoughts of what a something *should* be, you finally allow for that something to be what it is. What are the shoulds I am prepared to change right now?

My answer/quote:

_____
_____
_____
_____
_____
_____
_____
_____

My meaningful action:

_____
_____
_____
_____
_____
_____
_____

Suzanne Letourneau

My WHY:

_____

_____

_____

_____

_____

_____

_____

_____

SOAR with Heart-fullness

Day 21. *Meaning*-full is doing a simple action that leaves you feeling full-*filled*.

My answer/quote:

_____
_____
_____
_____
_____
_____
_____

My meaningful action:

_____
_____
_____
_____
_____
_____
_____

Suzanne Letourneau

My WHY:

_____
_____
_____
_____
_____
_____
_____
_____

Day 22. Meaning-*less* is when you feel a sense of less or discontentedness from your higher self after doing a particular action. When did I feel the most disconnected today?

My answer/quote:

My meaningful action:

Suzanne Letourneau

My WHY:

_____
_____
_____
_____
_____
_____
_____
_____

SOAR with Heart-fullness

Day 23. Your beliefs are just stories and your stories are just beliefs. They are one and the same. What are some of my limiting beliefs?

My answer/quote:

_____
_____
_____
_____
_____
_____
_____
_____

My meaningful action:

_____
_____
_____
_____
_____
_____
_____
_____

My WHY:

_____
_____
_____
_____
_____
_____
_____
_____

SOAR with Heart-fullness

Day 24. Beliefs are thoughts that you keep on replaying in your mind over and over again. Change the verse and you will have a new song. Change your thoughts, change your life. *(Day 24 & 25 work together.)*

My answer/quote:

_____
_____
_____
_____
_____
_____
_____
_____

My meaningful action:

_____
_____
_____
_____
_____
_____

My WHY:

_____
_____
_____
_____
_____
_____
_____
_____

SOAR with Heart-fullness

Day 25. Beliefs are thoughts that we don't question anymore. What if I would start questioning each one of my thoughts before they even become a belief?

My answer/quote:

_____
_____
_____
_____
_____
_____
_____
_____

My meaningful action:

_____
_____
_____
_____
_____
_____
_____
_____

Suzanne Letourneau

My WHY:

_____
_____
_____
_____
_____
_____
_____
_____

SOAR with Heart-fullness

Day 26. What is your ultimate gift? What is your inspiration? Am I fulfilling my mission with the gifts I have been offered?

My answer/quote:

_____
_____
_____
_____
_____
_____
_____
_____

My meaningful action:

_____
_____
_____
_____
_____
_____
_____
_____

Suzanne Letourneau

My WHY:

_____
_____
_____
_____
_____
_____
_____
_____

SOAR with Heart-fullness

Day 27. You have a limousine for the day. What do you do? Where do you go? Who is with you?

My answer/quote:

_____
_____
_____
_____
_____
_____
_____
_____

My meaningful action:

_____
_____
_____
_____
_____
_____
_____
_____

Suzanne Letourneau

My WHY:

_____
_____
_____
_____
_____
_____
_____
_____

SOAR with Heart-fullness

Day 28. In stillness resides your aliveness. What do you feel in your aliveness?

My answer/quote:

_____
_____
_____
_____
_____
_____
_____

My meaningful action:

_____
_____
_____
_____
_____
_____
_____

Suzanne Letourneau

My WHY:

_____
_____
_____
_____
_____
_____
_____
_____

SOAR with Heart-fullness

Day 29. A wizard offers you your long-time dream. What will it be?

My answer/quote:

_____
_____
_____
_____
_____
_____
_____
_____

My meaningful action:

_____
_____
_____
_____
_____
_____
_____
_____

Suzanne Letourneau

My WHY:

_____
_____
_____
_____
_____
_____
_____
_____

SOAR with Heart-fullness

Day 30. The world does not create what we are experiencing. We do. Why do I choose what I choose?

My answer/quote:

_____
_____
_____
_____
_____
_____
_____
_____

My meaningful action:

_____
_____
_____
_____
_____
_____
_____
_____

Suzanne Letourneau

My WHY:

_____
_____
_____
_____
_____
_____
_____
_____

SOAR with Heart-fullness

Day 31. We are the creator of our own life. What would I like to change in my life right now?

My answer/quote:

_____
_____
_____
_____
_____
_____
_____

My meaningful action:

_____
_____
_____
_____
_____
_____
_____

Suzanne Letourneau

My WHY:

_____
_____
_____
_____
_____
_____
_____
_____

SOAR with Heart-fullness

Congratulations! You have completed your 31 days of true introspection. Now, you want to focus on it for the rest of the year. No matter when you started, whether in January, May or September.

As of tomorrow, you go back to day one of this list, read what you wrote, feel it and, center yourself on that commitment for the rest of the day. Then go to day two, day three, day four, etc. Keep on doing this for the next 31 days.

Once you have reached 90 days, including those 31 days of writing your commitments, it is time for your first quarterly **assessment/inquiry.**

The inquiry is something to look forward to. It is a dynamic process into making discoveries and exploring your *wonder*-land!

Chapter 2
First Quarter

Assessment/Inquiry

It is now time to evaluate your commitments. This is a time for reflection, NOT a time for judgment. **Assessment/inquiry** means just that. The inquiry questions everything you have done so far toward your commitments, and the assessment guides you in the adjustments that need to be done. It is tweaking time!

In business, a quarterly review generally provides an update of all three financial statements: the income statement, the balance sheet and the cash flow statement.

In our assessment/inquiry we will look at three components also:

- Have you succeeded in accomplishing some of the 31 meaningful actions, commitments that you have outlined in your plan? It is not the quantity that counts but the quality of your actions. Make a list and remember, no accomplishment is too small.

_____
_____
_____
_____
_____
_____
_____

- What did you find the most challenging? Breaking a long-time habit, changing limiting beliefs or stepping out of your comfort zone are some of the most difficult things to do. But once you do, it becomes one of the most inspiring.

_____
_____
_____
_____
_____
_____

- What was the most fulfilling? In what way?

_____
_____
_____
_____
_____

Chapter 3
Second Quarter

Assessment/Inquiry

Half of the year has come and gone. How are you doing? Dive into your wonder-land and remember, this is a time for reflection, NOT a time for judgment.

As mentioned before, in business, quarterly reviews generally provide an update of all three financial statements: the income statement, the balance sheet and the cash flow statement.

However, the number that the business owner is looking forward to the most is the **earnings,** as quarterly earnings provide the owner with an overview of sales, expenses and net income.

In this second quarter, it is time to provide an update for all three components.

And most importantly, we will look at the *L-earnings*.

- Which of the 31 commitments have you been able to absorb pretty easily?

- Which did you find the most demanding? How did you handle it? Please be clear and precise on the how. It will help you for the rest of the year.

SOAR with Heart-fullness

- Which was the most fulfilling? How?

_____
_____
_____
_____
_____
_____
_____

The ***L-earnings*** are kind of your **aha** moments. What is **aha** moment? It's official definition is "a moment of sudden realization, inspiration, insight, recognition, or comprehension." What have you suddenly grasped, realized or understood at a deep level and, that you are now going to incorporate into your life?

_____
_____
_____
_____
_____
_____
_____

Suzanne Letourneau

"What difference does the content of a belief make in one's life?"

Chapter 4
Third Quarter

Assessment/Inquiry

Only 3 months left before the end of the year or before the end of your 12 month commitment. Wow! Where did the time go?

Let's look at the three components:

- Have you succeeded in accomplishing half of your 31 commitments? Make a list of the ones that are still outstanding.

_____
_____
_____
_____
_____
_____
_____
_____

- What are you finding the most difficult and why? How can you change your perception on this task?

Suzanne Letourneau

_____
_____
_____
_____
_____
_____
_____
_____

- What was the most fulfilling, inspiring? How has it changed your life so far?

_____
_____
_____
_____
_____
_____
_____
_____

The assessment/inquiry would not be complete without the ***L-earnings***.

SOAR with Heart-fullness

What have you cheerfully realized and understood in a profound way that you have started to integrate into your life on a daily basis?

_____
_____
_____
_____
_____
_____
_____
_____

Chapter 5
Fourth Quarter

Assessment/Inquiry

This is your last review before the year-end assessment. Very exciting isn't?

How has your life changed? How different do you feel? Let's take a look:

- What are the remaining commitments that are still outstanding? Make a list. Why are you resisting them?

_____
_____
_____
_____
_____
_____
_____
_____

- What do you find so demanding about them? You have created those commitments, after all. What limiting belief of yours is stopping you from attaining your goal?

_____
_____
_____
_____
_____
_____
_____
_____

- What was the most fulfilling/rewarding? How?
  (Once again, be very clear about the whole thing.)

_____
_____
_____
_____
_____
_____
_____

SOAR with Heart-fullness

The *L-earnings*

_____
_____
_____
_____
_____
_____
_____
_____

**"Are you unconsciously unconscious
of your gifts,
your blessings your unique calling?"**

Chapter 6
Year-End

Bravo! You did it.

This is the moment you have waited for.

A whole 12 months of intense work, focused inquiries and honest assessments. It is now time to collect your earnings! If you have done your quarterly assessment with *earnest* attention, which I have no doubt you have, you must hold a pretty clear idea on how things are going with your **L-*earnings***: Commitments - Meaningful Actions - **W.H.Y**.

We will address the year-end slightly differently, as the year-end is all-ways the stepping stone for the following year: review, adjust, change, eliminate, or continue and add more of the same great stuff.

Therefore, we also want to look at your investments.

The investments on what you have created, how you have created it and, why you did. This also involves looking at the missed opportunities and why you are keeping old commitments that are not serving you at all.

Once again, I remind you that a <u>commitment is a choice</u>. A choice that YOU make.

YOU are the process for everything that happens in your life. YOU are the basis for every relationship that you have, including the biggest one, the one with your-*self*.

It is NOW the time to choose to be in alignment with your own knowing, your true and higher knowing. So let's do this. Let's look at the three components once again and this time I need you to go deeper into the investments that you have made: **how painful it was,** or **how pleasant and relieving it was, how disturbing it still is** or **how comfortable it has become** and **how distressing** or **uplifting, it now, is.**

This is surely your biggest assessment of the past 12 months. I have no doubts you can do it.

Make a brief and concise list for each one of the components.

Assessment/Inquiry

My answer/quote:

_____
_____
_____
_____
_____
_____
_____

My meaningful action:

_____
_____
_____
_____
_____
_____
_____

My W.H.Y:

_____
_____
_____
_____
_____
_____
_____

My L-earnings:

_____
_____
_____
_____
_____
_____
_____

SOAR with Heart-fullness

Overview

Commitment is a choice. Vision is a choice.

Are your choices in alignment with the life you want for yourself?

We see what we want to see. We hear what we want to hear.

Change what you want to see, and what you see will change.

Change what you want to hear, and what you hear will change.

Change your thoughts, change your life.

Shift your perception, stop the pain.

Invest your energy in meaningful thoughts and actions.

The meaningless world will end as the illusion it is.

About the Author

Suzanne Letourneau was born and raised in Montreal, Qc, Canada. Her quest for a spiritual connection to all around her led to extensive travel and the experiencing of many cultures, religions and philosophies.

She has co-authored three books: *Adventures in Manifesting – Health & Happiness*, *The Unstoppable Woman's Guide to Emotional Well-Being* and *Empowered Women of Social Media*. But it is in her award-winning book *SOAR with Vulnerability – Eleven Insights to the Full Enjoyment of your Life* that you will find her most powerful message.

SOAR with Vulnerability is the first in a series of SOAR books that are now being followed by her current book, *SOAR with Heart-Fullness – Keys to a Meaningful Life,* and others. The SOAR movement also includes workshops and seminars for individuals and companies, as well as one-on-one private coaching.

When asked why she does what she does, Suzanne's answer is simply: "*I exist to inspire others to truly experience life and live truthfully. Get Curious. Be Outrageous.*" She constantly challenges you to step out of your comfort zone to explore new possibilities in vulnerable authenticity.

If you want to contact the author, you can email her at: suzanne@suzanneletourneau.com
or visit her website: http://www.suzanneletourneau.com/

www.ingramcontent.com/pod-product-compliance
Lightning Source LLC
Chambersburg PA
CBHW071300040426
42444CB00009B/1810